CHICAGO

PARK DISTRICT EMPLOYEE RETIREMENT GUIDE 2025

(SECOND EDITION)

ILLINOIS PUBLIC PENSION FUND ASSOCIATION

FOREWORD BY
JAMES MCNAMEE
PRESIDENT

WINDY CITY PUBLISHERS

Chicago Park District Employee Retirement Guide

2025 (Second Edition)

Windy City Publishers
www.windycitypublishers.com

Printed in the United States of America

ISBN:
978-1-953294-71-5

Library of Congress Control Number:
2024913255

Windy City Publishers
Chicago

To Chicago Park District Employees,
active and retired,
who have faithfully served
all Chicagoans

Illinois Public Pension Fund Association
An Association of Public Pension Funds
2587 Millennium Drive, Unit C
Elgin IL 60124, 630-784-0406
www.ippfa.org

CONTENTS

DISCLAIMER

INFORMATION APPEARING ELSEWHERE

Some of the information presented appeared earlier in books by IPPFA project coordinator and author Dan Ryan. Permission has been given to use this information in this retirement guide for Chicago Park District employees, but the writings were solely created by the authors and are the property of the authors.

GENDER REFERENCES

Efforts have been made to make the content of this book gender neutral. When the phrase "he" is used, it is done sparingly and only for the purpose of conversational flow of the text.

BULK PURCHASES

This book is available on Amazon.com and by bulk purchase (minimum 10 copies) from the IPPFA Office. Contact us at (630) 784-0406 to inquire about bulk purchases.

FOREWORD

SINCE 1985, THE ILLINOIS PUBLIC Pension Fund Association (IPPFA) has committed time and resources to assist local fire and police pension boards in administering benefits and investing funds to help public safety professionals achieve a secure retirement.

Along the way, we expanded our efforts to ensure that individual members had the ability to maximize their own retirement security and success. As part of that effort, in 2021 we published a retirement income guide for suburban and downstate Illinois police and firefighters.

This was followed early in 2024 by publishing the same type of guide for Chicago police and fire professionals. Now, this new book is another tool in that ongoing effort. It brings together much of the information needed to understand and fully utilize retirement income benefits available to Chicago Park District employees. We trust that it will fulfill every reader's needs.

Please remember that beyond this information, there is no limit to the opportunity to expand your personal knowledge of both the financial aspects of life after you stop working as well as the non-financial issues that you may face in retirement. Public sources (books, articles, websites, etc.) on these matters are virtually unlimited. Don't let your pre-retirement and post-retirement education end with this book.

And a great source is your pension fund office, the Parks Employee's Annuity and Benefit Fund of Chicago (chicagoparkpension.org). Your retirement fund has a full-time professional staff, and excellent website and active and engaged trustees elected by you or appointed by the District.

Note that at the time of publication, there is discussion about necessary changes in the benefit levels for Tier 2 retirees—those workers who first became Parks employees after January 1, 2011. When you begin to seriously consider your retirement income, please check with the Chicago PEABF office to verify your Tier 2 benefit levels.

Finally, and most importantly, thank you for your commitment to the people of Chicago.

~James McNamee
President
Illinois Public Pension Fund Association
August 2025

INTRODUCTION

YOUR RETIREMENT INCOME IS DIFFERENT

Retirement income is often said to resemble a three-legged stool. It may consist of a pension, Social Security, and your personal savings. Each of the three legs, in your case, is different than the retirement structure of a private-sector worker.

Like you, a neighbor who works at Motorola® or a brother who is a union plumber have pension plans that contribute to retirement security. But their pension plans are formed and governed under the federal Employee Retirement Income Security Act (ERISA). The Pension Benefit Guarantee Corporation (PBGC) provides a base level of insurance should their private sector plans become insolvent. The Board of Trustees has broad latitude to set benefits. It is unlikely that there is any payroll deduction to fund a portion of the benefit—their plan is fully paid for by the employer. There are strict rules protecting the pension rights of spouses, both those married to the pensioner and those who are divorced.

As for your pension, the environment and structure are very different. Chicago Park District pensions are *not* governed by ERISA or insured by any federal agency. Your pension trustees do not set benefits; the State of Illinois does. There is no pension "plan"—there is a pension law adopted by the legislature and signed by the governor. *And you, the employee, pay a substantial portion of your own pension via payroll deduction*—a fact sometimes missed or understated by politicians, citizens, and the media.

As to other aspects of retirement income, your friends and relatives most likely participate in the Social Security system at work. You do not. When you spend thirty years outside of Social Security, your federal benefits are greatly impacted. Fortunately, the 2025 *Social Security Fairness Act* eliminated formulas and offsets that previously affected the benefits that a Park District retiree might receive from Social Security. But you are still outside that system for your peak earnings years.

Your personal savings rules are also different, at least those that govern tax-advantaged savings at work. Private corporate workers save through a 401(k) plan, charitable and educational groups through the 403(b). You save under Section 457 of the Internal Revenue Code. Over the past decade, Section 457 rules have come very close to the 401(k) structure, but there are still differences. A news story or a public television show on workplace savings may not be fully applicable to you.

The purpose of this book is to explain your retirement benefits as they apply to *you*, Chicago Park District employees. We'll look at each leg with emphasis on your unique situation as a public employee in Chicago.

The first chapter of this book discusses the Illinois pension provisions that provide retirement income to Chicago Park District employees under Article 12 of the Illinois Pension Code.

A chapter follows on Social Security. The Social Security material is written for people who are outside of that federal system for public service (*i.e.* Chicago park employees).

The next chapter covers the opportunities for the "personal savings" leg of your retirement plan made available through Deferred Compensation under Internal Revenue Code Section 457.

This material is concise but thorough. It doesn't cover every law, rule or other element of retirement income, but it does hit the key areas that affect Chicago park employees. Any questions remaining? Please contact your very capable pension office, deferred compensation administrator (Empower Retirement), or contact us at IPPFA.

Illinois Public Pension Fund Association
Elgin, Illinois
August 2025

1

CHICAGO PARK DISTRICT PENSIONS

OVERVIEW

Persons employed by the Chicago Park District receive retirement and disability benefits from the Park Employees' and Retirement Board Employees Annuity and Benefit Fund (PEABF). The benefits, fund structure, and required member contributions are all spelled out in Article 12 of the Illinois Pension Code. This Article may be found in the Illinois Compiled Statutes, Act 5 of Chapter 40, Article 12 at the following link:

https://www.chicagoparkpension.org/about-us/.

This chapter explains the pension benefits payable to Chicago Park District retirees and survivors covered under the Article 12 PEABF system.

MEMBERSHIP

> *Any person who becomes an employee of the Chicago Park District (or "CPD") is required to be a member of the Fund as a condition of employment, provided they are employed in a position that requires the person to work six months or more per calendar year.*

In 2010, the Illinois Legislature created a two-Tier Benefit System. Employees hired prior to January 1, 2011, or who were contributing members of a reciprocal public pension fund prior to January 1, 2011, are Tier I employees. Employees hired on or after January 1, 2011, and who were not contributing members in the Chicago Park District Fund or a "Reciprocal Fund" prior to January 1, 2011, are Tier II Employees. On August 6, 2021, the Illinois Governor signed House Bill 417 creating a third tier, Tier III, of pension benefits for employees hired after January 1, 2022. Any new hire with the Chicago Park District that has contributed to any designated Reciprocal Retirement System before January 1, 2022, may be eligible for the benefit plan under Tier 1 or Tier II. Tier 2 members were given a window to irrevocably elect to be Tier III members from January 1st, 2022, through April 1, 2022.

CONTRIBUTIONS BY EMPLOYEES

For Tier 1 and Tier II membership, a contribution of 9% is deducted from a participant's gross salary. 7% is allocated to an employee for retirement pension; 1% for the surviving spouse's pension; 1% for the post-retirement increase in the retirement pension. For Tier III membership, a contribution of 11% is deducted from a participant's gross salary. 9% is allocated to an employee for retirement pension; 1% for the surviving spouse's pension; 1% for the post-retirement increase in the retirement pension. Please note that for all purposes the term "spouse" refers to marriage spouse and civil union spouse.

A deduction of $3.60 per month is also taken for the Single Sum Death Benefit.

Tier II and Tier III employees have a limit on their pensionable salaries that was set by law, and which is increased by the Consumer Price Index-U (CPI-U). The salary limitation for Tier II and Tier III members can be found at:

https://insurance.illinois.gov/Applications/Pension/Default.aspx

PURCHASING PAST SERVICE

An employee hired before January 1, 1992, may purchase the 6-month pre-entry period after 10 years of service or after attaining age 60, whichever first occurs. An employee can purchase previously refunded contributions from the Fund if a member has been contributing to the Fund for at least 2 years after being rehired. A member can purchase additional service, service with the Park District that was not paid into the Fund previously. Additional service can only be purchased by members who have contributions in the Fund. Members must contribute to the Fund for at least 2 years to purchase additional services. All past service must be paid prior to retiring from the Fund or any Reciprocal Fund. Employees may have the option to purchase military service. Please contact the Fund for more information.

CONTRIBUTION AND BENEFIT TAXATION

Employee contributions are excluded from the employee's gross taxable income. Federal income tax is deferred until the employee receives retirement benefits, obtains a refund after withdrawal from service or upon the death of an employee or an annuitant. Retirement and surviving spouse's pensions are not currently subject to Illinois state income tax.

CONTRIBUTIONS BY EMPLOYER

Beginning in 2022, the Chicago Park District **is** required to make contributions calculated on an actuarial basis to ensure the Fund is 100% funded within 35 years. This means that an independent actuary determines the amount the CPD would contribute to the Fund on an annual basis based upon a number of financial factors such as the Fund's assets, liabilities, investment returns, participant life expectancy and other economic and demographic factors. The revenue from the CPD contributions along with the employee contributions and income from investments, are used to cover the cost of benefits provided by the Fund.

REFUND OF CONTRIBUTIONS

An employee who terminates CPD employment before qualifying for a pension is entitled to a refund of employee contributions only, without interest. For Tier 1 employees, the refund is payable to an employee who withdraws before age 55, regardless of length of service. It is also payable to an employee who withdraws after age 55 and before age 60 with less than 10 years of service and to an employee who withdraws at age 60 or over with less than 5 years of service. For Tier II and Tier III employees, the refund is payable to an employee who withdraws before age 62 and age 60, respectively, regardless of length of service. It is also payable to an employee who withdraws with less than 10 years of service, regardless of age. An employee not meeting these conditions has no right to a refund and must accept a pension.

MEMBERSHIP RECORD

Each participant must file with the Fund, an accurate membership record showing date and place of birth, marital status and family information, such as name of spouse and names and dates of births of children. Please be sure to update your records in the event of your marriage, divorce or birth/adoption of a child.

BENEFICIARY

A participant must name a beneficiary or beneficiaries (using a Designation of Beneficiary Form) to receive a refund of the employee's pension contributions and/or the Single Sum Death Benefit in the event of death. This form may be obtained from the office of the Fund or the Fund's website. Please be sure to update your records in the event of your marriage, divorce or the death of a designated beneficiary.

COMPUTATION OF SERVICE CREDIT

Generally, 9 months or more of service during a year (January 1 to December 31) are counted as one year of service; 6 to 8 months inclusive, ¾ of a year; 3 to 5 months inclusive, ½ of a year; less than 3 months, ¼ of a year; with 15 days or more during a month counted as a month of service. A month of service consists of working at least 45 hours per month.

RETIREMENT PENSION

An employee must submit an application for pension with the Fund in order to receive any benefits. Applications must be completed and submitted prior to the proposed termination date. If not, the date of receipt will be the date used as date of retirement. An employee, who is a member of the Fund, is entitled to a retirement pension based on a fixed benefit formula. The current percentage rate that applies to all credited years of service is 2.4%, and this accrual rate applies to all retirements (or termination from service) on or after December 31, 2003. The 2.4% will be multiplied by the member's years of service to formulate an overall pension rate (the maximum is 80% with 33.5 years of service). This total percentage (years of service multiplied by 2.4%) will be applied to the "final average salary" as described below.

The following illustrates the specific pension requirements:

	Tier I	**Tier II**	**Tier III**
Retirement Eligibility -Minimal	10 years of service and 50 years of age	62 years of age with 10 years of service (discount applies regardless of years of service if under age 67)	60 years of age with 10 years of services (discount applies regardless of years of service if under age 65)
	4 years of service and 60 years of age, member has an option to either refund their contributions or take a monthly pension		
	5 years or more of service and 60 years of age, member is locked into a monthly pension		
	Mandatory pension benefit applies if member is over age 55 with 10 or more years of service (discounted if under age 60)		
-Full (non-discounted)	Age 60 or over with 5 years of service, or age 50 or over with 30 years of service	Age 67 or over, with 10 years of service	Age 65 or over, with 10 years of service
	Maximum pension is 80% of average salary with 33.5 years of service	Maximum pension is 80% of average salary with 33.5 years of service	Maximum pension is 80% of average salary with 33.5 years of service

	Tier I	Tier II	Tier III
Average Salary Computation	Based on the highest 48 consecutive months over the last 10 years of service	Based on the highest 96 consecutive months over the last 10 years of service	Based on the highest 96 consecutive months over the last 10 years of service
Computation of Discount	If retiree is under age 60 with less than 30 years of service, a discount of ¼ of 1% for each month retiree is under age 60	If retiree is under age 67 a discount of ½ of 1% for each month retiree is under age 67	If retiree is under age 65 a discount of ½ of 1% for each month retiree is under age 65
Salary Limitations	Total gross salary received, exclusive of overtime, F-time or V-time is used in the computation of average salary	In addition to Tier 1 limitations, the earnings for pension calculation purposes are limited based on the Illinois Department of Insurance.	In addition to Tier 1 limitations, the earnings for pension calculation purposes are limited based on the Illinois Department of Insurance

POST RETIREMENT INCREASE IN RETIREMENT PENSION

Any employee receiving a lifetime benefit will be entitled to an annual increase based on the annuity granted at the time of retirement. Depending on the Tier of a participant, the specifics of post-retirement increases are detailed in the chart on the next page:

	Tier I	**Tier II**	**Tier III**
Eligibility for Annual Increase	Age 60 or over	Age 67 or over	Age 65 or over
	Age 50 with at least 30 years of service		
Requirement	Payable following the first 12 months of benefits on either the next January 1st or July 1st	Payable following the first 12 months of benefits on the next January 1st	Payable following the first 12 months of benefits on the next January 1st
Rate	3% of granted annuity (fixed)	Not to exceed 3% of granted annuity and subject to ½ of the unadjusted percentage increase in the Consumer Price Index-U (calculated yearly)	Not to exceed 3% of granted annuity and subject to ½ of the unadjusted percentage increase in the Consumer Price Index-U (calculated yearly)

SURVIVING SPOUSE'S PENSION

A surviving spouse is the employee's spouse member on the date of retirement and/or death, if death occurs prior to retirement. The surviving spouse is entitled to a pension upon the death of an employee while in service or upon retirement. If the surviving spouse remarries before attaining age 55, the spousal annuity is canceled. Based on the Tier of a participant/annuitant, the specifics of the surviving spousal pension are detailed in the chart on the next page:

	Tier I	Tier II	Tier III
Passing of Annuitant			
- Less than 20 years of service	Spouse is entitled to the lesser of: • A money purchase calculation • 50% of highest salary • 75% of granted pension	66 2/3% of the benefit being received by the participant/annuitant at date of death	66 2/3% of the benefit being received by the participant/annuitant at date of death
- 20 or more years of service	The greater of the above computed entitlement or 50% of the annuitant's benefit at time of death		
Passing of employee	See computation for "Passing of Annuitant", with possible reductions due to age of surviving spouse	66 2/3% of the annuity earned by the member at date of death, without a reduction due to age of surviving spouse	66 2/3% of the annuity earned by the member at date of death, without a reduction due to age of surviving spouse
Annual increases	3% compounded increase at each January, subsequent to one full year after the date of death of the participant or annuitant	Lesser of 3% simple or ½ CPI-U increase at each January, after the first anniversary of granted annuity	Lesser of 3% simple or ½ CPI-U increase at each January, after the first anniversary of granted annuity

CHILDREN'S PENSION

Regardless of Tier status, unmarried children under the age of 18 of a deceased employee having at least 2 years of service are entitled to a pension. If one parent is living, the pension is $100per month. If no parent survives, the pension for each child is $150 per month. The total amount payable to a surviving spouse and/or children may not exceed 60% of the employee's final salary except where the employee's death resulted from death on duty.

SINGLE SUM DEATH BENEFIT

A lump sum death benefit is payable upon the death of an employee in service. The amount payable is as follows:

- $ 3,000 benefit during the first year of membership
- $ 4,000 benefit during the second year of membership
- $ 5,000 benefit during the third year of membership
- $ 6,000 benefit during the fourth through ninth year of membership
- $10,000 maximum benefit after 10 or more years of membership

Upon retirement, the $10,000 maximum benefit is reduced to $6,000 if death occurs during the first year of retirement. Thereafter, it is reduced by $1,500 for each year or fraction of a year while on retirement but shall not be less than $3,000. Upon retirement with less than 10 years of service, the death benefit payable is the amount shown for the years of membership less $1,500 for each year or fraction of a year while on retirement but shall never be less than $3,000. Please note, by law no death benefit is payable unless the employee's retirement application was made within 60 days from the date of withdrawal from service.

The death benefit is payable to a surviving spouse. If there is no surviving spouse, it is payable to a designated beneficiary. If there is neither a surviving spouse nor a designated beneficiary, it is payable to the employee's/annuitant's estate.

ORDINARY DISABILITY BENEFIT

This benefit is payable to an employee medically certified as disabled after eight (8) consecutive days' absence without pay, who was in actual service or salary status prior to the disability. Payment begins subsequent to the completion of the required form from the first day of sickness. The payment is 45% of salary. In addition, a credit is made to the employee's pension account of an amount equal to the pension contribution the employee would have made while working. The benefit is payable for a period of time not to exceed ¼ of the employee's credited service or 5 years, whichever is less. (Note: An employee who is out of pay status for more than 30 days and re-enters service will not qualify for ordinary or duty disability benefits for 6 months unless he or she was qualified to receive the ordinary or duty disability benefit before he or she left pay status).

DUTY DISABILITY BENEFITS

Employees who become disabled as a direct result of an injury on duty with the CPD are entitled to a duty disability benefit of 75% of salary. Employees are entitled to the duty disability benefit from the first day of absence without pay.

The duty disability benefit is offset by any total temporary disability benefits received under the Workers' Compensation Act. The portion of the disability benefit payable by the Fund will be suspended upon the filing of an application for adjustment of claim with the Illinois Workers' Compensation Commission. If, upon resolution of the application, the Workers' Compensation payments exceed the 75% duty disability benefit, then the portion of the duty disability benefit will not be paid by the Fund and the employee will be required to repay any duty disability benefits received from the Fund.

If, upon resolution of the application, the Workers' Compensation payments do not exceed the 75% duty disability benefit, then the portion of the duty disability benefit will be paid by the Fund. In addition, the pension contribution account is credited with the amount the employee would have contributed while at work. The employee shall also receive an additional benefit of $20 per month for each eligible minor child. The combined payments together with the pension credit may not exceed the monthly salary rate at date of disability. This benefit is payable during disability until the employee attains age 65 if disability is incurred before age 60 or for 5 years if disability is incurred at age 60 or older.

DUTY DISABILITY DEATH BENEFIT

Upon the death of an employee resulting from an accident incurred in the performance of duty, the surviving spouse is entitled to a benefit of 50% of salary and a monthly payment of $100 is made for each unmarried minor child under 18. The combined payments to a family may not exceed 75% of the employee's final salary, reduced by Workers' Compensation payments. Pension credits for the regular pension to a spouse continue to accumulate during the period of payment of the duty disability death benefit.

PENSION CREDIT FOR OTHER RETIREMENT SYSTEMS, MILITARY SERVICE, OR FEDERAL GOVERNMENT SERVICE

An employee who has accumulated pension credit with another retirement system covered by the State of Illinois' Reciprocal Act may make use of this credit for pension purposes. See the Appendix to this Chapter for more information on the Reciprocal Act and a list of the participating funds. The PEABF Office has a two-page brochure that describes in more detail how the Reciprocal Act works. It is available through their website at chicagoparkpension.org.

In addition, an employee may purchase additional pension credit for military service and/or periods of employment by the United States Federal Government. Contact the Fund Office for additional information regarding these credits.

QUALIFIED ILLINOIS DOMESTIC RELATIONS ORDER ("QILDRO")

Effective July 1, 1999, the Fund recognizes QILDRO's that permit an alternate payee to receive a portion of a member's pension benefits. Specific rules must be followed to properly implement a QILDRO. Contact the Fund Office for additional information regarding the processing of a QILDRO.

BEFORE YOU RETIRE, PLEASE CONSIDER:

- Federal tax laws periodically change and may affect the taxability of your pension.
- Participation in the CPD's deferred compensation plan could supplement your retirement income. See Chapter 3 for more information on Chicago Park District deferred compensation.
- Are you eligible for Social Security from work outside of the PEABF system or through a spouse? See Chapter 2 for an expanded explanation of your opportunity for benefits under Social Security.

These and other issues should be considered well in advance of retirement. You should also consult your tax advisor.

Should you have any questions, contact the Fund Office at 312-553-9265, 3500 S. Morgan Street, Suite 400, Chicago IL 60609.

GOVERNANCE

Legal Creation and Oversight

As noted in the introduction to this Chapter, Illinois law governs your Article 12 pension fund. Federal law plays only a small taxation and disclosure role. The Illinois Pension Code is Chapter 40 of the Illinois Compiled Statutes, 40 ILCS 5, and then the specific pension systems are created and regulated under separate articles. The Chicago Park Employees' Annuity & Benefit Fund of Chicago is one of those specific pension systems.

The Board of Trustees and Staff

The Fund is governed by a Board of Trustees ("the Retirement Board") consisting of seven members: four elected by the employees and three appointed by the Chicago Park District Board of Commissioners. The Trustees have a fiduciary responsibility to govern the Fund in a prudent manner consistent with the requirements of Illinois law. Meetings are held monthly and are open to the public except when personnel matters are discussed or similar allowable topics, as permitted by Illinois law.

The Fund has a professional staff who assist the Trustees in operating the pension plan and give aid and guidance to Chicago Park District employees and retirees.

Website—www.chicagoparkpension.org

The Fund maintains an excellent website at www.chicagoparkpension.org. You can get general information from the site as well as request a pension estimate and download forms. This is especially important if you need to update your Membership Record or Designation of Beneficiary Form. Be sure to complete the entire form and have it *notarized* (if required) before submitting it to the Fund. The website also has the following features:

ANNUAL REPORTS

Fully transparent reporting on the annual audit, actuarial valuation and investment performance.

THE "STEPS TOWARD RETIREMENT"
A document detailing the actions you need to take to begin the retirement application process and the timing of pension benefits.

RECIPROCAL BROCHURE
This document describes the opportunity to merge service between the Chicago Park District PEABF pension benefit and twelve other public pension funds throughout the city and state.

www.Chicagoparkpensions.org is a great resource—use it!

Role of Professional Consultants

To assist the Board of Trustees in carrying out their duties, the Fund retains a qualified actuary, certified public accountant, an investment consultant, investment managers, a custodian bank and independent legal counsel.

Role of the Illinois Department of Insurance

The Department of Insurance is authorized under the statutes to create rules governing pension administration, to regulate public pension funds, to audit public pension funds, and to report to the Legislature as to the valuation of these funds. The Public Pension Section handles these responsibilities. The entire department and the pension section are active participants in protecting public employee pensions. They may be contacted at the Public Pension Section, Illinois Department of Insurance, 320 W. Washington St., Springfield, IL 62767.

Required Participant Information

As previously noted, to ensure coverage and benefits under the Pension Fund, CPD personnel should complete the pension plan's necessary forms. Note that the State of Illinois requires that information on marital status, children, and your birth certificate be kept in the pension fund's records. If your information is always up to date, this will help ensure timely processing of your benefits, especially if a catastrophic event occurs. Also, since it is a requirement of the pension fund that this data be maintained, keeping your records current will help your pension fund when they are examined by the State.

Administrative Review

Final administrative decisions of the Board of Trustees are subject to judicial review under the Illinois Administrative Review Law.

WANT MORE INFORMATION?

As discussed, the PEABF website at www.chicagoparkpension.org has excellent on-line information for active and retired participants. You can also gain access to the plan's financial information. The audit and actuarial reports are quite detailed but are worth the effort for you to learn about your pension fund. Also, the actuarial report has an excellent summary of benefits that you can use to supplement your knowledge about your pension benefits.

Contact the PEABF professional staff to assist you with any questions at 312-553-9265, 3500 S. Morgan Street, Suite 400, Chicago IL 60609.

As a Chicago Park District employee, you are not covered under Social Security during your employment. However, you may have earned Social Security benefits from work outside of public employment. Be sure to read the section of this book on Social Security benefits.

Also, you are eligible to voluntarily save and invest a portion of your salary under the Park District's Section 457 Deferred Compensation Plan. Read the section of this book on deferred compensation and contact your plan provider, Empower Retirement, at 1-800-701-8255 for specific information.

If you have service under one of the Reciprocal Funds, see the Chapter Appendix that follows and be sure to contact the other fund to confirm your service credit and to coordinate your retirement with both PEABF and the Reciprocal Fund.

CHAPTER 1 APPENDIX — LIST OF RECIPROCAL FUNDS

The Illinois Retirement Systems Reciprocal Act (Reciprocal Act) gives retiring Illinois public employees the option to combine service credit earned in most Illinois public retirement systems (Chicago and other local police and fire funds are excluded). The Chicago Park District's PEABF is one of the thirteen Illinois public retirement systems covered by the Reciprocal Act.

If you elect to retire under the provisions of the Reciprocal Act, your service from each pension plan is combined upon retirement. The total combined service credit is then used to determine your eligibility for pension benefits from each system and the amount of those benefits. Participation in reciprocity is not required. If you choose to retire under the provisions of the Reciprocal Act, the systems will exchange information to determine your pension benefits. The PEABF Office has a brochure on the Reciprocal Act that describes in more detail how pension service between two (or more) funds can be coordinated. It is available at their website, chicagoparkpension.org.

Reciprocal Act Participating Systems

Park Employees' Annuity and Benefit Fund of Chicago
3500 S. Morgan Street, Suite 400
Chicago, Illinois 60609
Phone: 312.553.9265
Fax: 312.553.9114
www.chicagoparkpension.org

Chicago Teachers' Pension Fund
425 S. Financial Place, Suite 1400
Chicago, Illinois 60605-1000
General: 312.604.1400
Members: 312.641.4464
Fax: 312.641.7185
www.ctpf.org

County Employees' Annuity and Benefit Fund of Cook County
70 W. Madison Street Suite 1925
Chicago, Illinois 60602-3103
Phone: 312.603.1200
Fax: 312.603.9760
www.cookcountypension.com

Forest Preserve District Employees' Annuity and Benefit Fund of Cook County
70 W. Madison Street Suite 1925
Chicago, Illinois 60602-3103
Phone: 312.603.1200
Fax: 312.603.9760
www.cookcountypension.com

General Assembly Retirement System
2101 S. Veterans Parkway P.O. Box 19255
Springfield, IL 62794-9255
Phone: 217.782.8500
Fax: 217-524-9039
https://ilsrs.illinois.gov/gars.html

Illinois Municipal Retirement Fund
2211 York Road Suite 500
Oak Brook, Illinois 60523-2337
Phone: 800.275.4673 or 630.368.1010
Fax: 630-706-4289
www.imrf.org

Judges' Retirement System
2101 S. Veterans Parkway
P.O. Box 19255
Springfield, Illinois 62794-9255
Phone: 217.782.8500
Fax: 217-524-9039
https://ilsrs.illinois.gov/jrs.html

Laborers' Annuity and Benefit Fund of Chicago
321 N. Clark, Suite 1300
Chicago, Illinois 60654
Phone: 312.236 4700
Fax: 312.236.0574
www.labfchicago.org

Metropolitan Water Reclamation District Retirement Fund
111 E. Erie Street, Suite 330
Chicago, Illinois 60611-2898
Phone: 312.751.3222
Fax: 312.751.5699
www.mwrdrf.org

Municipal Employees' Annuity and Benefit Fund of Chicago
321 N. Clark Street, Suite 700
Chicago, Illinois 60654-4767
Phone: 312.236.4700
Fax: 312.236.2383
www.meabf.org

State Employees' Retirement System (SRS)
2101 S. Veterans Parkway
P.O. Box 19255
Springfield, Illinois 62794-9255
Phone: 217.785.7444
Fax: 217 785-7019

SRS Chicago Office
Michael A. Bilandic Building
160 N. LaSalle Street, Suite S200
Chicago, Illinois 60601
Phone: 312.814.5853
Fax: 312.814.5805
www.state.il.us/srs

State Teachers' Retirement (TRS) System
2815 W. Washington Street
P.O. Box 19253
Springfield, Illinois 62794-9253
Phone: 877.927.5877
Fax: 217.753.0394

TRS Lisle Office
4200 Commence Court, Suite 101
Lisle, Illinois 60532-3611
Phone: 630.505.0071
Fax: 630.505.9607
www.trsil.org

State Universities Retirement System (SURS)
1901 Fox Drive
P.O. Box 2710
Champaign, Illinois 61825-2710
Phone: 800.275.7877
Fax: 217.378.9800
www.surs.com

2

SOCIAL SECURITY FOR CHICAGO PARK DISTRICT EMPLOYEES

UP UNTIL RIGHT NOW, 2025, there were provisions of the Social Security Act that reduced benefits for retirees who had pensions from work outside of Social Security. These two provisions, the Windfall Elimination Provision (WEP) and the Government Pension Offset (GPO) were repealed in early 2025 by an act of Congress and signature by the President. The law, the *Social Security Fairness Act*, is retroactive to January 2024. So, as you read this updated chapter, the same Social Security laws and formulas now apply to you as they do to every other worker in the country.

In previous books and other training material, IPPFA provided a detailed explanation of the WEP and the GPO. This is no longer necessary, and they are not addressed in this update, other than to emphasize their repeal. Instead, we now provide a basic overview of Social Security and instructions on where to go for more detailed information.

During the discussion, this chapter alternatively uses the familiar "SSA" for Social Security, as in Social Security Act or Social Security Administration.

WHAT'S UP WITH SOCIAL SECURITY IN ILLINOIS?

Quite a few public employees do not participate in Social Security for their government work. Chicago employees, related agencies like the Park District, most suburban and downstate police and fire, the State University system, CPS and other Illinois teachers and Cook County employees do not participate in Social Security. But most of these people will earn a Social Security check from private sector work before, during (part-time), and after their public service careers. The monthly check that these workers will receive from Social Security will be lower than the benefits paid to typical American workers. This is because these cops, firefighters, teachers and Park District workers spend twenty-plus years of their peak earning time outside of the Social Security system.

WHY ARE MOST ILLINOIS PUBLIC EMPLOYEES OUTSIDE OF SOCIAL SECURITY?

Pretend that you could travel back to 1787 Philadelphia. You would observe thirteen guys sitting around a table at Independence Hall banging out a draft of what would become the US Constitution. A big issue then was the relationship between the federal and state governments. Nobody wanted the federal level to be superior. After the debate was over, the national government was given some express and strongly implied powers, and the rest were left to the states explicitly or generally under the 10th Amendment.

It seems kind of quaint and outdated now, given that the national government can use highway money to get the states to change speed limits. But this concept of *federalism* is still a guiding principle of our country; the national government and the states are both sovereign and draw their powers from a constitution. Affairs within a state are generally left to the state.

Does this have anything to do with the fact that Chicago fire and police or Park District employees don't pay into Social Security? Actually, yes. When SSA was established, state and local government employees were excluded from participating due to concerns about constitutionality. The employer-employee relationship was considered to be purely a state affair (and thus beyond the role of the national government). Also, the employer "match" under FICA was seen as a tax on one level of government by another.

In time, constitutional concerns abated and amendments to SSA allowed the states to participate if the employee group was not covered by a stand-alone retirement system. Eventually each of the fifty states entered into agreements with the Social Security Administration that defined who would or would not be covered by Social Security.

In Illinois, Chicago and related agencies were excluded from SSA participation, along with many other public employees.

SOCIAL SECURITY BASICS

SOCIAL SECURITY WAS ESTABLISHED IN 1935 as part of the New Deal legislation following the Great Depression. By 2024, it was paying just over $1.4 trillion in annual benefits, the largest program in the federal budget. The system provides base-level retirement, disability, and survivor benefits to most American workers. It is sometimes referred to as a social insurance program, intended to keep people above the poverty level. Social Security is funded by employee contributions from the paycheck, an employer match of the same amount, and taxation on Social Security benefits. The long-term projections for funding of the system show a need for improvement either in revenue (higher taxes), a larger contribution base, benefit modifications, or some combination of the three. Private, individual-accounts as a future for Social Security have been discussed but not received favorably.

In the future, even if the Social Security trust fund balance drops to zero, worker and employer contributions and taxes would cover approximately 77% of future benefits. This is certainly a gap that America can manage. It's not productive for people to proclaim that *"Social Security is not going to be there for me."* It will be.

THE BASICS

WHO PAYS FOR SOCIAL SECURITY?

Workers pay 6.2% of their covered earnings for Social Security benefits and 1.45% for Medicare. Their employer matches those same payments. Wages over a certain level ($176,100 in 2025) are not taxed but are also not included in any benefit calculation. All workers, including those not in SSA, pay the 1.45% Medicare tax if they were hired after March 21, 1986. Virtually all Illinois and Chicago public servants are paying for Medicare and will be entitled to that retiree medical benefit when they turn 65.

You've seen the Social Security deduction taken out of your paycheck when you worked in SSA covered employment. It appears under the heading "FICA." This stands for Federal Insurance Contribution Act, the part of the Social Security legislation that sanctions the payroll deductions.

How Does Someone Earn a Benefit?

You are eligible for a Social Security benefit after you earn forty "credits" in the system. A credit is earned by receiving a certain amount of Social Security covered wages in a year. In 2025, the amount was $1,810 for one credit (it was lower in the past, will be higher in the future). Up to four credits can be earned in one year, so the requirement is sometimes called "forty quarters" as opposed to "forty credits." Forty quarters is almost 100% accurate, but a schoolteacher on a summer break could make a little over $7,200 and earn four credits during a single calendar quarter.

Two general truths result from this. First, it takes ten years of elapsed time in Social Security to earn a benefit. Second, it's not that hard to qualify for at least a small benefit. Even if you are out of SSA for thirty years at the Chicago Park District, there is still time before, during and after that to earn a small amount of SSA-covered wages and get your forty quarters/credits. Most people in Illinois public service are entitled to or are on track to be entitled to Social Security benefits. You can tell if you have earned a benefit if you received a statement from Social Security telling you so. These statements are sent to participants at age 60 but are available online before and after that age if you have registered a personal "my Social Security" account at ssa.gov.

What Benefits are Earned?

Social Security benefits are paid to recipients, generally, in one of four forms:

> *Retirement* benefits from a worker's own record of Social Security earnings;
>
> *Spousal* benefits from a spouse's record while the spouse is still alive;

Survivor benefits from a spouse's record after the spouse has died;

Disability benefits if you can no longer work due to illness or injury.

It is important to note that a recipient may only receive one type of benefit at any one point in time. A person who receives a Survivor benefit gives up his or her own retirement benefit. A public pension fund does not work this way. If a married couple are both retired as Article 12 Chicago parks retirees, when one dies the survivor may receive a survivor pension as well as her own retirement pension. This is not allowed with Social Security benefits.

BEYOND THE BASICS

RETIREMENT BENEFITS FROM YOUR OWN EARNINGS RECORD

Let's look first at how Social Security retirement benefits are calculated using the worker's own record of earnings under Social Security. This is the way that most Social Security benefits are paid, as opposed to disability, spousal and survivor benefits.

REPLACEMENT RATES, FINAL SALARY, AND SOCIAL SECURITY

Remember your Chicago Parks Pension. Your benefit is calculated based on the salary at the end of your career, which is then multiplied by a percentage factor based on your years of work. This percentage is called the "replacement rate" (*i.e.*, the portion of your salary that is replaced by your pension). So, 80% of final pay for thirty-three and one-half years of service, 48% for twenty years of service, or 75% for line-of-duty disability reflect replacement rates of 75%, 48%, and 75% respectively multiplied by final pay.

Social Security uses the same concept with two fairly major deviations. The first difference is how the salary for the computation is determined. The second is that varying replacement rates are used on different portions of your earnings. It's a bit complicated, but understandable.

Salary Used for Social Security Calculation

In the Illinois Article 12 Chicago Park pension system, the salary used for the Tier 1 pension calculation is essentially the final four years of salary. In Social Security, it is the highest 35 years, *almost the entire working life of a person.* But, because some of those wages were earned so long ago, the Social Security formula adjusts (*i.e.,* indexes) those wages to inflation. Thus, if a person who retired in 2024 earned $10,000 back in 1989, Social Security indexes those wages forward to $26,916 when they calculate the person's average indexed earnings over his or her 35-year total.

A notable truth, especially for parks personnel and other Chicago workers: calendar years with no SSA earnings ($0) count when calculating the average earnings. Consequently, if a worker had inflation adjusted earnings of $15,000 yearly for five years, then no Social Security earnings during a 30-year public service career ($0), then $50,000 annually for ten years, his or her average indexed earnings over the highest 35 years would be as follows:

10 years at $50,000	$500,000
5 years at $15,000	$75,000
20 years at $0	$0
Total—Highest 35 Years	$575,000
Average over 35 Years	$16,430
Indexed Monthly Average—35 Years	$1,369

Replacement Rates

After the average salary is calculated (called "average indexed monthly earnings" or AIME), the SSA system then uses different replacement rates for up to three separate levels of an individual retiree's indexed income. For persons attaining age 62 in 2025, those income levels and replacement rates are:

First $1,226 in monthly earnings	90%
Next $6,165 in monthly earnings	32%
Over $7,391 to taxable maximum	15%

Let's look at an example of how these rates work for three different Social Security recipients:

MONTHLY AVERAGE WAGE	CALCULATION	BENEFIT	REPLACEMENT RATE
Retiree #1—$800	$800 @ 90%	$720	90%
Retiree #2—$1,600	$1,226 @ 90% $374 @ 32%	$1,223	76%
Retiree #3—$8,500	$1,226 @ 90% $6,165 @ 32% $1,109 @ 15%	$3,242	38%

Notice the progressive nature of Social Security benefits (lower income earnings receive a higher percentage replacement). The very low paid worker gets 90% of pay in Social Security benefit. The highest paid worker shown gets some at 90%, most at 32%, and a portion at 15%. The highest wage earner's final replacement rate is 38%. That 38% doesn't appear anywhere in the published formulas—it's a weighted compilation of the three different published rates of 90, 32, and 15 percent.

ESTIMATING YOUR OWN BENEFIT

What does this mean for a Chicago parks system retiree? Your earnings in Social Security covered employment will likely be somewhat sparse, and your benefit will be lower than your private-sector friends and relatives. Using the example of a person with lifetime index earnings of $1,369 shown earlier in the book, the Social Security benefit amounts to $1,149 at the Full Retirement Age (more on the FRA later). If you earned higher average earnings during your working life in Social Security, your benefits will be higher. Earn less than that amount, the benefit will be lower.

A superior approach is for everyone to go to the *ssa.gov* website and register for an account for access to their own private information. Once you have registered, you can examine your own record and run projections based on your earnings to-date and your estimated Social Security earnings in the future.

The good news is that since the Windfall Elimination Provision (WEP) has now been repealed, your benefit will be higher and the opportunity to estimate your own Social Security benefits is the same as every other worker. Previously it was necessary to download your earnings record from ssa.gov and then input the data into a special WEP Calculator. That is no longer needed.

SOCIAL SECURITY BENEFITS FROM YOUR LIVING SPOUSE'S RECORD

In general, a retiree receives Social Security benefits equal to (a) the benefits earned from his own work record or (b) one-half of his spouse's Social Security benefit, whichever is higher. Two examples follow:

Mark's SSA Benefit	$2,000
Sue's SSA Benefit from her own record	$800

Sue will receive the following:	
From her own record	$800
From Mark's Record	$200
Sue's Total Benefit	**$1,000**

Sue is entitled to her own SSA benefit plus a spouse's benefit so that her total Social Security payment is one-half of Mark's. Together, the couple will receive $3,000 (Sue's share does not come out of Mark's benefit). A second example:

Ward's Benefit	$2,200
June's SSA Benefit from her own record	$0

June will receive the following:

From her own record	$0
From Ward's Record	$1,100
June's Total Benefit	**$1,100**

June was at home taking care of her two sons and never worked enough time in SSA covered employment to accumulate forty credits, so she has no benefit on her own record. But she is still entitled to benefits from Ward's record of earnings. Together the couple will receive $3,300.

THE GOVERNMENT PENSION OFFSET (GPO)—REPEALED

Previously, the Government Pension Offset provided for a reduction in Social Security benefits *from a spouse's record* of 66-cents for every dollar a City of Chicago or Park District employee received from a municipal pension. At the time, examples weren't really needed since the GPO usually eliminated any benefit payable under a living spouse's record.

But, as noted, the GPO has now been repealed. A Chicago parks employee may receive an unreduced Spousal benefit if his or her own earned benefit is less than one-half of the spouse's Social Security benefit.

Is a Spousal Benefit Helpful for a City of Chicago or Parks Employee?

The advantages of the now unrestricted Spousal benefit will vary among Chicago government workers. For some city workers who are outside of Social Security for most of their careers, there may or may not be an advantage. If your spouse was a full-time parent for many years and earned only a modest

Social Security benefit on her earnings, your own benefit may be more than one-half of hers (even though you were outside the Social Security system for decades). This would leave no Spousal benefit available for you.

However, if your spouse worked mostly full-time in Social Security covered employment, one-half of his or her benefit may be a little more, somewhat more or *much* more than your own Social Security. Under those circumstances, a Spousal benefit will be advantageous for you. The good news is that the Social Security application process examines both benefits, your own and any Spousal benefit, that you may be entitled to.

SOCIAL SECURITY BENEFITS AS A SURVIVING SPOUSE

In retirement, a surviving spouse can collect up to 100% of the late spouse's Social Security benefit. There are also Survivor benefits available prior to retirement, with age and/or dependent child rules that apply. About 3.8 million widows and widowers were receiving Survivor benefits as of August 2024 (source: AARP).

However, in retirement, a surviving spouse gives up his or her own Social Security benefit once a Survivor benefit is paid. This is different than a public pension system. If a married couple consists of two retired Chicago parks workers, when one dies the other can continue the retirement pension and be paid a survivor benefit from the Chicago parks pension plan. Not so with Social Security.

Previously, just like the Spousal benefit, the Government Pension Offset provided for a reduction in Social Security *Survivor* benefits. This rule no longer applies. It is now more likely that a Chicago parks retiree will receive a Social Security Survivor benefit than before, but this is not guaranteed. Remember that if your own Social Security benefit is higher than your wife or husband's, no Survivor benefit will be paid to you because your own benefit is higher.

A WORD ABOUT DIVORCE

Both Spousal and Survivor benefits are available based on the earnings record of an ex-spouse as long as the marriage lasted 10 years and the recipient remains unmarried. This is a special circumstance and should be personally explored if it may affect you. However, at the time of retirement, the Social Security application process should bring this opportunity into the calculation of a Spousal or Survivor benefit.

A WORD ABOUT DISABILITY BENEFITS

In addition to retirement and survivor benefits, Social Security also provides disability benefits. However, the definition of disability under Social Security may be harder to meet than the definition under the Illinois Article 12 Chicago parks pension system.

In addition to meeting the Social Security definition of disabled, a worker must have had Social Security covered wages within a timeframe established by Social Security in order to receive disability benefits. If you qualify, the SSA benefit will be fairly small since your earnings exclude your parks system professional wages. Still, that small monthly disability check could still provide a person with critical income at a time when it is sorely needed.

SOME WORDS ABOUT CLAIMING STRATEGIES

All of us will be faced with decisions regarding when and how to receive our Social Security benefit. There is a fancy phrase for this—a claiming strategy. It was always an important subject, but with the repeal of the Government Pension Offset, there are now more claiming possibilities for retired public service employees.

At the simple end of the spectrum is the issue of what age to begin taking the benefit. A retiree can begin as early as age 62 (with some limits on allowable wage income) or may defer as late as age 70. With each month of delay, the benefit goes up. A retiree and spouse might make different decisions on the age at which to draw SSA benefits. In this approach, some income starts to flow into the household, but some is deferred to a later age (with the money growing each year it is deferred).

The information that follows touches on some of the basic information needed to develop a claiming strategy. Neither IPPFA nor the authors are experts in this subject, and advice on how to access the necessary expertise will follow.

Full Retirement Age (FRA)

The FRA is the age at which the calculated benefit (shown in the prior charts and examples) is payable to the retiree. In Social Security parlance this is called the Primary Insurance Amount (PIA). Your Full Retirement Age is shown on the following chart:

Year Born	Full Retirement Age
Thru 1954	66 years old, 0 months
1955	66 years old, 2 months
1956	66 years old, 4 months
1957	66 years old, 6 months
1958	66 years old, 8 months
1959	66 years old, 10 months
1960 and later	67 years old

Claiming Before your Full Retirement Age

You can claim your Social Security benefit as early as age 62. If you claim before your Full Retirement Age, the benefit is reduced each month that you draw before your FRA. Examples of the reduction amount based on an FRA of 67 years old follow:

Claiming Age	Reduction
62	30.0%
63	24.9%
64	20.0%
65	13.1%
66	6.7%

In addition to experiencing a reduction in the monthly payment, persons who draw their Social Security before their Full Retirement Age are subject to an annual limit on wages and self-employment income. If the retiree exceeds the limit, their Social Security is reduced in the following year by 50-cents for every $1 that the limit was exceeded. In 2025, that annual wage limit is $23,400. This is an indexed amount so it will be higher in years after 2025. Note that the income limit is higher in the calendar year that you actually reach the FRA.

Deferring Social Security

You may also defer your retirement benefit after your Full Retirement Age. If you do so, your benefit goes up each month by a uniform increase of 8% per year (prorated monthly). Examples based on an FRA of 67 follow:

Claiming Age	Increase in Social Security
67	Calculated Benefit
68	8% higher
69	16% higher
70	24% higher
71 and above	No further increases

What's the Best Age to Draw?

Whether there is a "best age" or not is subject to debate. There is a lot of material written and easily available on this subject. Overall, delaying your Social Security makes sense if you are going to live longer than the average American. You will receive the higher amount for more months and years.

Generally, the formulas are "neutral" based on system-wide life expectancy. Under such neutrality, if Maddie draws at 62, Mike at 67 and Mandy at 70, they all are making a good decision if it fits their needs.

While the formulas are based on system-wide life expectancy, public employees generally have educations levels at high school or above, middle class incomes and health insurance while they are working. These are all drivers of increased life expectancy. Also, many public employees have passed medical and physical examinations in order to get their jobs. In short, your life expectancy is likely better than that reflected in the Social Security calculations.

Also, the reduction formulas do not take gender into account. Since women live longer than men, women should consider delaying their Social Security.

One possible approach: if you need the money, then begin taking Social Security. If you don't need it, delay so that your benefit is higher in your later years and any potential Survivor benefit you leave to a spouse will be higher.

Other Claiming Considerations

There may be the opportunity for some married couples to coordinate their Social Security claiming to their advantage. One spouse can begin drawing on their own benefit and then later switch to a Spousal benefit when their spouse retires.

A more complicated issue involves a retiree applying for his or her benefit but then suspending immediate receipt. This was allowed previously, but a new law quashed this benefit claiming opportunity for anyone who wasn't 62 by January 2nd of 2016. When it was allowed, the approach permitted the spouse to begin collecting a Spousal benefit off of the retiree's record. Later, that spouse could switch to benefits under his or her own SSA record, which would have grown each year the benefit was deferred up until age 70. For many workers and spouses, "file and suspend" could have presented some very nice alternatives. But the opportunity is now gone for most retirees.

Serious consideration of claiming strategies is beyond the scope of this chapter. There is a lot written on this subject, available free online. You can also engage the services of an expert, in person or online, to run specific strategies based on your (and your spouse's) actual Social Security record. You could spend a few hundred dollars at most but be guided to a strategy worth more than $100,000 over a couple's lifetimes.

Two services that have been examined by the authors are listed below. IPPFA does not endorse any provider, but these services appeared to be thorough and reasonable in cost. They are:

> **MaximizemySocialSecurity.com.** This is the website of a Boston University professor and author on benefit maximization. It is recommended by Terry Savage, a nationally syndicated columnist.
>
> **SocialSecurityAdvisors.com**. They provide a very complete report as well as an option to speak to an expert.

Also, if you have a personal financial advisor, that individual may have advanced software that can assist you in making a claiming decision.

SOCIAL SECURITY WRAP UP

CHAPTER SUMMARY

There is a lot of information in the chapter you just read. Let's summarize where we have traveled:

Social Security benefits are based on a worker's wages over his or her working life, essentially 35 years. Forty credits (usually ten years) must be earned to obtain any benefit.

City of Chicago and Chicago Park District employees are not covered by Social Security while in City employment. Still, they are likely to earn Social Security benefits from work before, during, and after their public careers. They will generally earn a lower benefit than their neighbors and friends because of the many high-wage years they spend outside of Social Security.

Prior to 2025, special rules applied to the benefit calculation of persons who earned pensions outside of Social Security covered employment. Those rules, the Windfall Elimination Provision (WEP) and the Government Pension Offset (GPO) were repealed upon adoption of the *Social Security Fairness Act.* Because of this change, there is a higher likelihood that Chicago Park District retirees will earn benefits under the Spousal and Survivor benefit allowances.

The "three-legged stool" of retirement income includes pension, Social Security, and personal savings. For most Illinois public employees, the Social Security leg will be lessened by a career outside of Social Security. Their generally higher pension benefits than the private sector workforce are designed in part to make up for this lower Social Security benefit.

IS SOCIAL SECURITY PARTICIPATION VALUABLE?

Yes. There is almost always a benefit to earning Social Security covered wages. If a job opportunity presents itself, either part-time or after your parks system retirement, there is no reason not to pay the 6.2% payroll deduction and qualify for or earn a higher monthly benefit.

This applies across the board. For a new parks employee who only has a few years in Social Security before coming to the Park District, it will pay in the long run for him or her to gain forty (40) credits/quarters and qualify. For someone who has already achieved Social Security eligibility and is retiring from the public employment, adding to their Social Security record prior to attaining age 62 or even later will add to their retirement income.

And, as discussed above, active employment in Social Security can qualify a person or increase benefits should he or she become disabled.

SOCIAL SECURITY PUBLICATIONS.

Social Security has numerous publications available for download (or audio listening) from their website, ssa.gov. A few publications that may help in providing an overall view of Social Security are listed below. Some of these publications need to be updated to remove any reference to the WEP and the GPO. If you run across these provisions, don't worry about them. Recommended publications are:

Understanding the Benefits
Publication #05-10024, January 2024
Get an overview of all Social Security programs and Medicare.

Retirement Benefits
05-10035, January 2024
Learn about Social Security retirement benefits: how you earn coverage; how to apply; how benefits are figured; and how to decide when to retire.

Your Retirement Benefit: How It Is Figured
05-10070, January 2023
Learn about the formula used to calculate Social Security retirement benefits and take advantage of a worksheet to help you estimate your retirement benefits.

Disability Benefits
05-10029, March 2024
People with disabilities can get basic information on Social Security benefits.

ANYTHING ELSE?

Again, you should consider opening up an account with Social Security (ssa.gov) to at least view a statement of earnings and benefits estimates or go further to see your entire record and run your own estimates.

When you get to retirement, become your own expert on the issue of claiming strategies or find a professional online or in person to assist you.

As the Social Security Administration works to implement the *Social Security Fairness Act* (and the elimination of WEP - GPO), persons already receiving Social Security benefits will have a big interest in SSA's progress on these changes. Overall, Social Security has done a good job.

For those of you who are not yet collecting Social Security, their systems should be able to accurately handle your application when you apply in the future.

For those who are already collecting, the *Act* is retroactive to January 2024. It will take time for the Social Security Administration to fully re-calculate all benefits and make retroactive payments. At the date of this publication, they have made considerable progress. Social Security had the following information on their website. The website, www.ssa.gov/benefits/retirement/social-security-fairness-act.html, will be updated from time to time.

> **If you have previously filed for Social Security benefits and they are partially or completely offset,** at this time, you do not need to take any action except to verify that the Social Security Administration has your current mailing address and direct deposit information if it has recently changed. Most people can do this online by accessing their personal Social Security account without calling or visiting a Social Security office.

> **If you have not previously filed for Social Security benefits,** you are receiving a public pension and you are interested in filing for benefits, you can file for benefits online at ssa.gov or schedule an appointment.

Most retired Chicago and other Illinois employees who are age-eligible for Social Security benefits have applied for and are receiving benefits. However, there will be some public employees who *never applied* for benefits because they did not have forty credits, and their pension would have totally offset any Spousal benefit. Social Security is now recommending that they apply for benefits.

Finally, good luck on making the most of your Social Security benefits upon the passage of the *Social Security Fairness Act.*

IPPFA, August 2025

3

PUBLIC EMPLOYEE DEFERRED COMPENSATION

WHAT IS DEFERRED COMPENSATION?

When a person receives wages (*i.e.*, compensation), income taxes are withheld, and the amount earned is reported to the IRS at the end of the year.

However, sections of the Internal Revenue Code (IRC) and Illinois law allow an employee to *defer* receipt of some wages on a pre-tax basis until after he or she retires. At the time these deferred wages are earned, they are neither received in the paycheck, subjected to tax withholding, nor reported as taxable to the IRS (unless a Roth option is chosen, which is explained later). The money instead is deposited into an account and invested as directed by the employee. When the accumulated dollars are ultimately received after retirement (or sooner in some cases), the withdrawal payments are then reported to the IRS as taxable distributions. This deferral of wages and taxes until after retirement is commonly referred to as deferred compensation or "deferred comp."

For most public employees, deferred compensation under IRC code Section 457 is the strongest part of the "personal savings" leg of the three-legged retirement income stool (pension, Social Security and personal savings). Your personal savings can of course include the value of your home, brokerage accounts, individual retirement accounts, investment real estate, and bank savings. But the ability to save through the paycheck on a tax-advantaged basis has made deferred compensation a large personal asset for many public employees. For this reason, and because your deferred compensation operates a little differently than your neighbor's 401(k) plan or your nurse-sister's 403(b), Section 457 savings is the focal point of the chapter of personal savings for Chicago Park District employees.

CHAPTER OUTLINE

In this chapter, we will first look at some background information on Section 457 plans. Then, we'll "follow the money." We cover how money is put into the plan, how it is invested along the way, and how it is withdrawn to meet your goal of a secure retirement. Regarding the middle part, this is not an investment guide. There is really nothing unique about 457 investing when compared to other supplemental plans where the employee self-directs the account. But we'll still go over the basics. Then the chapter ends with hopefully good tips for you on how to proceed, along with some final enthusiasm for these excellent plans.

LEGAL STANDING

Deferred compensation systems have evolved under legislation and IRS rulings specifically in relation to the employer of each worker. Each plan is designated by the section of the Internal Revenue Code that authorizes and governs the deferral. Section 401(k) plans, the most prominent type of deferred compensation, grew out of profit-sharing plans and have been primarily used by private sector employees in for-profit companies. Section 403(b) has been the primary plan for employees of education, scientific, and charitable organizations. These plans are found in many not-for-profit hospitals, and both public and private schools. Finally, Section 457 plans are available to employees of state and local government and, in a modified form, to some management and professional employees of not-for-profit agencies. We'll concentrate on the government form available to Chicago Park District employees.

HISTORY OF 457 PLANS

Prior to 1978, various organizations obtained "private letter rulings" from the IRS allowing public employees to defer compensation. An actual code section authorizing deferrals was subsequently included in the *Revenue Act of 1978* as a new Section 457(b) of the code. There have been revisions since then, the notable being the improvements in the 1996, 2000, and 2002 reform laws. Most importantly, the 1996 reform law established that funds held in a 457 plan are in a trust fund and are not available to the municipalities' general creditors. This change, long overdue, followed the bankruptcy of Orange County (California) after an investment scandal.

Changes in 2000 and 2002 went a long way in making 457 plans look more like its private sector cohorts under 401(k) and 403(b). The allowable contribution amounts were made to be very similar between the plans. The withdrawal rules and the opportunity for rollover from one plan to the other or to an Individual Retirement Account (IRA) were made similar. Prior to these reforms, it was very important for public sector employees to be given special instruction on 457 plan deferred compensation (the withdrawal rules were particularly complicated). That need has lessened now—public employees can obtain general information from the financial industry or media on deferred compensation and then check with their plan administrator for specific 457 plan rules.

The Chicago Park District has offered a deferred compensation plan for decades. The plan is administered by Empower Retirement. Specific information on the plan and various forms are available at empower.com or by calling 1-800-701-8255.

HOW DOES TAX DEFERRAL IMPROVE RETIREMENT SAVINGS?

In a traditional tax-deferred plan, an employee elects to defer compensation at a set amount or a percentage of pay. When he or she is paid each payday, the deferred compensation amount is deducted from the paycheck and deposited into a dedicated account. Taxes withheld from the paycheck are calculated on the basis that the amount deferred was taken from the paycheck "before taxes." So, the paycheck does not go down as much as the total amount put into the deferred compensation account. Then, at the end of the year, the amount deferred is not reported to the IRS or state as a taxable wage. An example follows.

A Tale of Two Savers

To see how pre-tax deferring compensation compares to savings through taxable channels, we look at two savers, Tim and Suzanne. They both earn $4,000 monthly and can afford to put away $300 per month for retirement savings. Tim opens a brokerage account for his investments and has his employer send the $300 to his account via the ACH automated banking system. Suzanne joins her public employer's deferred compensation plan. Here's how their monthly gross and take-home pay are affected (excluding Medicare or pension contributions, which are unchanged by either approach).

	TIM	SUZANNE
Salary	$4,000	$4,000
Deferred Compensation	0	(428)
Taxable Wages	$4,000	$3,572
Federal Tax	540	427
State Tax	200	185
Brokerage Account Deposit	300	0
Net Pay	$2,960	$2,960

Tim and Suzanne both have the same monthly net pay but Suzanne saves $428 monthly while Tim puts away only $300. This happens because Suzanne's tax deferral advantage on the $428 deposit reduces her net pay by only the $300 that she can afford. Of course, Tim is free and clear on the taxes for the principle amount he has saved; Suzanne eventually does pay the tax on her $428. But let's see how that works out.

Suppose Tim earns 7.5% annually on his savings and pays 23.1% in tax on his earnings each year. If he keeps up his savings/investment/tax program for 30 years, he'll have $281,200 in his account at retirement. If Suzanne earns the same 7.5% return over 30 years, her balance will accumulate to $551,000. She still owes tax on that amount, but she has almost twice the amount that Tim has. Tax rates are simply not high enough to take away the advantages she has already gained.

Also, there are other factors in her favor. First, if she lives in a state that doesn't tax 457 withdrawals, such as Illinois, she will avoid the state tax completely. Moreover, if she draws her money out gradually (while still experiencing investment earnings), she will continue to enjoy the benefit of tax deferral while drawing money out at levels that do not trigger excessive taxes.

Personal financial experts are virtually unanimous in their advice that deferred compensation is an excellent way to save. Even changes in the tax code, which reduced taxes for people who own stocks and mutual funds outside of deferred compensation, have not diminished the attractiveness of these plans.

NOTE

If an employee routinely pays a large amount of money to the IRS at year-end, enrolling in or increasing deferrals in a Section 457 plan may not eliminate a large tax payment on April 15th, although it will reduce it somewhat. The employee may still need to adjust his tax or her withholding by completing a revised declaration of exemptions (W-4), which is available from the payroll office.

What about the Roth approach?

There was a senator from Delaware named Roth who in 1997 got Congress to establish the Roth IRA. In time, which morphed over into a Roth 401(k) and eventually a Roth 457 option. Your employer, the Chicago Park District, does offer a Roth 457 option.

Most public employees save for retirement using a traditional tax-deferred 457 plan as opposed to a Roth. Because of that, we've concentrated this chapter of the book on the method that most of us have used. Also, the pros and cons of Roth savings are the same for you as for your IRA or 401(k) saving friends and relatives. So, you can get useful information from most sources that provide such advice.

But, in case this Roth thing is new to you, we provide just a short explanation. In a Roth 457 plan, there is no tax savings or other advantage at the time the employee makes his or her payroll deduction deposit. So if Suzanne in my example put $428 monthly into a Roth 457 plan, her pay would go down $428, not the $300 shown in the table. However, the money earned on Roth deposits is not taxed at the time of a qualified withdrawal. To be qualified, the withdrawal has to take place after age 59-1/2 and at least five years after the initial Roth contribution. If a withdrawal is taken before these two requirements are met, investment earnings would be subject to federal taxation (but not the principal amount deposited). So the earnings in a Roth account are not simply tax-deferred, they are *tax-exempt*—a superior tax treatment at the time of withdrawal.

To summarize, the Roth approach has no tax break at the time of the deposit, but *all* of the earnings are tax-exempt when qualified withdrawal rules are followed. Not just deferred, *exempt*. The traditional 457 approach gives the saver a tax break going in, essentially creating more money to be saved, but those tax-deferred deposits and all earnings are eventually taxed.

RULES FOR DEFERRING INCOME

A maximum of $23,000 may be deferred in 2024, which will be indexed to inflation in the future. There is no statutory minimum amount of deferral.

There is a provision of Section 457 that allows an employee to exceed the annual maximum, up to double the amount of the annual maximum, in the last three years prior to being eligible to receive a pension from the employer-sponsored retirement plan. The additional amount deferred is limited to dollars that the employee *could* have legally deferred in the past but did not. It is further limited to the annual amount for regular contributions. For example, if the employee could have deferred $7,500 in each year of his first ten years of employment ($75,000) but only deferred $45,000 during those years, he or she has $30,000 left that can be deferred in the last three years prior to eligibility for receipt of pension (in addition to the regular maximum but nor more than twice the annual maximum in total).

This extra allowance is nicknamed "**the Catch-up Provision**," since the employee is catching-up on deferrals that could have been made earlier in his career.

The 2000 reform law added an additional savings opportunity, the so-called "Age 50 Catch-up Provision." This provision allowed a person over age 50 to contribute an additional $1,000 in 2002, incrementally increasing to $7,500 in 2024. This additional amount cannot be contributed in a year when the standard Catch-up Provision is being used. This Age 50 allowance is not dependent upon the existence of "unused deferrals" in prior years. It is simply additional authority to defer salary.

Note that at the time of publication, federal regulations were being written to implement changes to the Age 50 Catch-up. As provided for in the enabling law, Age 50 Catch-up for persons earning above certain wages will only be allowed in a Roth option. Implementation has been delayed until 2026 as an administrative transition period. Check with the deferred compensation company regarding any limitations if you are going to execute an Age 50 Catch-up.

The Rule of 72

Catch-up provisions are okay. But, if you can afford to, it's so much better to put a little more money into deferred compensation during your career than a lot of money at the end. Let's explore that idea further and learn an important investment concept along the way.

The variables that affect how much you accumulate in deferred compensation are the amount you put in, your investment return, and how long the money stays on deposit. The time factor is huge. The longer the amount of time your money is on deposit, the more fantastic things happen to it.

There is a mathematical **Rule of 72**. An investor can take his or her expected rate of investment earnings and divide it into 72. The product of that division is the length of time in years that it will take the invested money to double in value. So, at an easy-to-use estimate of 7.2% annual investment return, money doubles every ten years (72 divided by 7.2% = 10 years). If $3,000 is invested, it will become $6,000 in ten years, $12,000 in twenty years and $24,000 in thirty years. If the rate of earnings is higher, say at 8%, money will then double every nine years, not ten. At thirty years the same deposits will have grown to not $24,000 but $30,000.

The Rule of 72 amplifies the importance of time. If a person made that same $3,000 investment three years earlier and had it on deposit for thirty-three years, the same one-time deposit of $3,000 at 8% will grow to $38,000—26% more than the same dollars invested for thirty years.

Remember Suzanne's accumulated $551,000. Say she increases her savings in the last three years by a total of $30,000 by "catching up" $10,000 each year. If she does this, her end-of-thirty-year total grows to $584,000. If she instead found a way to put in the additional $30,000 by saving $1,000 more in each of the thirty years of her participation, the balance at the end is $658,000. True story.

Time is your friend. Save as much as you reasonably can as early as you can. Capitalize on "The Rule of 72."

But You May Want to Catch-up to Save State Taxes

Although the Catch-up Provisions aren't hugely effective for long term savings, there is a short-term advantage: money withdrawn from Section 457 plans in Illinois is not subject to state taxes. So, a participant can save 4.95% on his or her money going into the plan (since it's not subject to Illinois withholding or reporting) but state taxes are not assessed on the money when it is withdrawn. Thus, state taxes are not just deferred, they are eliminated completely. This is true on all your deferred compensation deposits and earnings if you remain an Illinois taxpayer and the law is not changed.

DEFERRED COMPENSATION—INVESTMENT OVERVIEW

This is an area in which you are not different. Any book, article or advice from an expert that educates you about asset allocation for retirement savings works for Section 457 plans.

Like the 401(k) plan, most Section 457 plans, including Chicago Parks, offer a variety of investments in the form of either public mutual funds or commingled investment accounts managed by investment experts. A participant can select from fixed or guaranteed rate investment accounts, various stock accounts, government and/or corporate bond accounts, or blended or balanced accounts that offer a combination of stocks, bonds, and short-term investment instruments. Your investment is held in trust and can only be used for your benefit under the rules of the plan and the Internal Revenue Code.

Since you can get advice or information anywhere and your investment goals and selections are not any different than your neighbor with a 401(k) plan, this book is not an investment guide. But we'll go over the basics, plus you may well have a certain amount of financial acumen anyway. You can then decide how much more research or assistance you need, if any, on this aspect of your personal savings and retirement plan.

Who Belongs in What Investment?

Professional investors break down the types of investments into broad asset classes—stocks, bonds, real estate, commodities, *etc.* How those are mixed together in a portfolio is called **asset allocation**. How does one select an asset allocation that is right for his or her long-term goals? You need to spend some time on this, as the experts say that asset allocation decision is far more important than which individual investments or funds that you select.

The American economic system rewards ownership. It is more advantageous to own a company than to lend the company (or a government) money, although lending certainly has its place in the economy and as an investment. When you invest in a stock mutual fund or other type of stock account, you are taking partial ownership of the many companies in the account. So, it is not a surprise that, by all historic measurements, stock market investments outperform other asset classes. Accordingly, the percentage of your asset allocation that you have in the stock market should be a key consideration.

The reality of investment returns supports the philosophical view of the benefits of ownership. Here are the various domestic market returns from January 1st, 1926 (before the Great Depression) to December 31, 2022:

Asset Class	**Annual Return**
Small Company Stocks	11.8%
Large Company Stocks	10.1%
U.S. Government Bonds	5.2%
30-Day U.S. Treasury Bills	2.9%

Source New York Life Investments—Ibbotson SBBI

Of course, such returns and those in the future may come with great volatility. Just look at what we've experienced over the past two decades: fantastic highs, retractions, periods of steady returns, two huge drops, and then big recoveries. But if you are a long-term investor, the long-term returns in stocks beat the safer bets, as long as you make some effort to manage the volatility, such as disciplined rebalancing.

Public Employees are Aggressive Investors

Both from the records of the IPPFA Benefits Division and anecdotally from other workers, we see that public employees tend to be fairly aggressive in their deferred compensation investing. That is, they have a relatively high percentage of their asset allocation in the stock market. They thus often capture more of the gains possible, *i.e.* those indicated in the preceding chart.

Whether these investors are less risk-adverse than the average investor or maybe just smarter, underlying this trend is a valid long-term saving concept. Because public employees are more likely to have a pension, *i.e.*, a guaranteed retirement income, they can take more risk with their separate, personal retirement savings.

100% Minus Your Age

If you prefer to be a little less aggressive, some personal financial experts suggest a basic formula known as **100% minus your age**. If you follow this formula, the percentage of your retirement assets that you will have in equities (*i.e.*, the stock market) will be equal to 100% minus your age. For example, if a person is 45 years old and subtracts his age from 100, the difference of 55 (*i.e.*, 55%) represents a suggested level for him to invest in stocks. If he was deferring $100 per paycheck, $55 would go to stocks and the balance would go to the bond or fixed accounts.

Using this formula, or a similar approach, a saver ends up investing more aggressively when he or she is younger. At age 22, "100% minus your age" puts 78% of money in stocks. Continuing, the formula reduces stock holdings as a person ages and ultimately approaches retirement. At age 60, only 40% of the money will be in stocks. This is what you may want to happen, because the amount of the portfolio that is in a volatile investment is reduced as retirement approaches. But you still maintain some opportunity for growth to beat inflation or hopefully a long life. Under this approach, even an octogenarian has 20% of her retirement account in the stock market.

Why Not 100% in Stocks?

Here is another math lesson. If I have a $1,000 stock investment that drops 25%, what do I have left? The answer is $750. This isn't too hard to figure out. But here is an important follow up question. What investment return do I then need to get my $750 back to $1,000 before I can grow my initial investment even by one penny? The answer is 33%, not the 25% I originally lost. Volatility is not just your investment going up and down—*volatility can hurt your returns.* That's why a 100% allocation to stock may be a little too risky.

Also, when the market is down for a prolonged period, your fixed income investments will help you keep your balances up *and* reinforce your confidence in deferred compensation. Further, placing a small portion of a portfolio in another asset class, even one that does not perform as well as your core investments, can result in less volatility and higher earnings if the account is rebalanced from time to time (more on that to follow).

Both of these factors are where the phase **diversification** comes in; you've heard that before. A variety of asset classes in your diversified portfolio keeps you almost whole when one asset class underperforms. You also can rebalance the asset classes to your long-term benefit.

Rebalancing

Very importantly, an allocation to both stocks and fixed income which you regularly rebalance will give you the opportunity to actually "buy low, sell high" for a long-term overall gain.

Let's say parks employee Addie is an avid deferred compensation investor and currently deposits her money each payday along a 60/40 stock/bond mix, with some of the stock piece in small companies and foreign stocks, and some of the fixed income piece to the plan's stable value fund. Over time, thanks to the pretty good performance in all aspects of her stock allocation, her account balance looks like this:

Small Company Stocks	$16,000	13%
Foreign Stocks	$8,000	6%
S&P 500 Index Fund	$59,000	46%
Bond Fund	$34,000	26%
Stable Value Fund	$11,000	9%
	$128,000	100%

Addie's stock allocation is now 65% of her portfolio even though her deposits went in at 60%. Good for her! She has been rewarded for her allocation to stocks. But she truly likes that 60/40 mix as part of her long-term goals and volatility management, so she rebalances the portfolio to look like this:

Small Company Stocks	$12,800	10%
Foreign Stocks	$6,400	5%
S&P 500 Index Fund	$57,600	45%
Bond Fund	$38,400	30%
Stable Value Fund	$12,800	10%
	$128,000	100%

She has been disciplined at rebalancing and transferred 5% of her money out of stocks and into bonds or fixed income investments, bringing her balance to the target 60/40 mix (as well as to her specific desired allocations within all stock and fixed income asset classes). Now, if the stock market or a specific portion of it drops, she has already captured some gains by transferring money out of stocks to bonds when stock values were higher.

Likewise, after the stock market has a bad year, she will rebalance bond money over to the stock side of her portfolio at the time that stocks are "cheap." Then when stocks recover, she will have more invested in stocks at the beginning of the rally.

A study published in *Forbes* in 2011 examined two hypothetical investors who each put $10,000 into a 60/40 mix of stocks and bonds in 1985. One never rebalanced the portfolio, the other rebalanced annually. For the entire 25-year period from 1985 to 2010, the portfolio of the investor who rebalanced grew to $97,000, beating the other investor at $89,000. Of course, there were times when the rebalancing didn't work, such as a prolonged bull market in stocks. But the theory and practice over the decades supported the concept of rebalancing a portfolio.

There are "balanced" fund and retirement date funds in your Chicago Park District 457 plan that automatically rebalance to their targets (see below). Or you can keep your eyes on your account and rebalance on a set schedule or just make a judgment call when you get a little or a lot off target.

Asset Allocation and Rebalancing Made Easy

A generation ago an investment adviser could conduct a two-day seminar on the why's and how's of proper asset allocation, diversification, and rebalancing. Then the major mutual fund companies and plan administrators came along with new products that execute these strategies automatically—the "balanced fund" or the "retirement date" fund or something similar. Balanced funds invest in a blend of assets that is routinely rebalanced. In a target or "retirement date" fund, the investor picks an approximate date for retirement, say 2050, then invests in a fund with that 2050 retirement goal in mind. That investment fund in 2024 is fairly aggressive in terms of its allocation to equities (stocks), including higher risk small companies and foreign stocks. But as 2050 approaches, the manager switches gradually to a more conservative portfolio. And, along the way, the account is regularly rebalanced. The Chicago Park District deferred compensation plan offers these balanced and retirement date funds.

A Word about Passive Investing

If you don't choose a target date fund but prefer to select your own investments, a well-regarded piece of advice is to invest some or a good portion of your savings in an index fund. Let's examine the idea of an "index" and then explore the concept and advantages of an index fund. Note that the Chicago Park District deferred compensation plan offers both stock index funds and a bond index fund as investment options.

An index is a hypothetical portfolio of investments that a knowledgeable group of people believe properly reflects the performance of an entire asset class. We hear about indexes all the time. When the TV news reports that the stock market went up 40 points, what does that mean? It means that a stock index, usually 30 companies monitored by the Dow Jones Company, went up 40 points. A broader index from Standard & Poor's tracks 500 large-company stocks; it is called the S&P 500 Index. When the stock market is measured over the years and decades, most observers are talking about the S&P 500. And there is an index for almost every asset class.

In 1976, the first "stock index fund" was launched, in which investor money was simply placed in each of the 500 S&P stocks. The fund did not have stock analysts researching whether any one stock, say Mobil Oil, was good deal. Mobil Oil (now Exxon) was in the index, so it was in the investment fund. Continuing, the index fund manager didn't consult economists to predict the ups and downs of the energy crisis. If 5% of the S&P 500 index companies were energy-related, then 5% of the index fund was in energy.

This is sometimes called passive investing. That phrase is used to differentiate the investment approach from an "active" manager who studies interest rates, company credit ratings, economic growth, and a zillion other factors before making an investment. The "passive" manager just sits back passively and selects securities that are in the underlying index.

This started in 1976. Today, there are trillions of dollars in index funds of all types: S&P 500, Wilshire 3000 small company index, Barclay's aggregate bond index, and many others.

Why invest in index funds? For two reasons: First, it's cheap. The fees charged against your investment balance in an index fund are the lowest available (your returns in public employee deferred compensation are always "net" of the fees paid to the investment manager). Since the index manager doesn't have to hire analysts and economists for the fund, those savings are passed on to the investor. Secondly, stock index funds, over time, produce returns comparable to or exceeding the more expensive "active" management approach.

But you may do better using active managers. Just keep the index concept in mind and do your own research into index or passive investing if the matter interests you.

How Safe is Section 457 Investing?

Risk of loss of principle is always present unless you are directly buying US government bonds or making FDIC insured bank deposits. Everything else includes some risk, such as a company going out of business or a foreign government defaulting on its debt. Only you can do both the research and the self-analysis to decide how much risk you are willing to take. The good news is that the various types of investment risk—credit, market, interest rates, foreign currency, whatever—are unchanged inside the Section 457 umbrella. Investing in the American Funds Growth Fund directly or through your 457 plan is no different, risk or otherwise.

How about out-and-out theft? Remember Bernie Madoff? He took investors' money, did *not* buy the securities or options that he promised, and then created phony statements to indicate that he had made proper investments. Meanwhile he was living the good life on his investors' cash. Could that happen in a major 457 administrator's operation or in the underlying mutual funds or accounts? Never say never, but it's just highly unlikely. All these operations have the proper trust account and custodian players in place (a custodian is a bank that holds the investments—the investment manager does not have access to the actual securities). If you have any doubts, talk to your plan representative.

We have a lot of confidence that the assets are safe. We know of no money that has been lost in modern day 457 savings other than from routine and expected investment volatility. The two principal authors of this book used the City of Chicago plan and a suburban government plan to build on their personal retirement security.

Closing Thoughts on Investing

Deferred compensation plans give a public employee the opportunity to build a diversified portfolio with an amazingly small starting investment. For example, a new participant in deferred compensation might have his or her first $20 deposit put one-fourth each into an S&P 500 index fund, a small company stock fund, an international stock fund, and a government bond fund. Is this really possible with just $20 —a $5 investment into foreign stocks and the rest into a diversified stock and bond portfolio? Yes, it is possible—in your employer-sponsored deferred compensation.

Allocation of retirement investment among asset classes is your most important decision after the decision to save, and before the decision of which specific mutual funds to pick. If you are unsure of how to invest your money, do some research or seek investment advice from a professional. Investing in a 457 plan is very similar to investing in a 401(k) plan, so investment advisers, good ones, should be able to help you.

A recommendation is either of two excellent books by William Bernstein: *The Intelligent Asset Allocator* and *The Four Pillars of Investing: Lessons for Building a Winning Portfolio*. Dr. Bernstein is a neurologist who at some point began to fancy himself to be an investment expert. Turned out he was right. You can use the excellent information in either of these books to assist you in your deferred compensation investment plan.

One way that a 401(k) plan and a 457 plan are dissimilar is that the 401(k) private sector employee may receive an employer match. The trade-off usually is that the private sector worker probably does not have a defined benefit pension like you do at Chicago Parks PEABF. But since you do have a defined benefit plan, here's something to remember: your fixed pension acts in many ways like a safe bond investment. If you consider that when you decide on an asset allocation in deferred compensation, you'll put considerably more in the domestic and foreign stock markets. The fact that your defined benefit pension plan pays out a guaranteed fixed amount each month allows you to be more aggressive in the stock market with personal savings.

Timing the market doesn't work. If you think you can *consistently* move out of stocks at the top and go back in at the bottom of the market, get out of parks and recreation work and make yourself a billionaire.

TURNING 457 MONEY INTO RETIREMENT INCOME

Section 457 money is deferred for retirement purposes. You do not have access to the funds until you either separate from employment (quit or retire), have an unforeseeable financial emergency, or participate in a loan program that is offered by your Section 457 deferred compensation plan.

The rules regarding withdrawal for an unforeseeable emergency are very strict. The emergency must be something for which a reasonable person would not budget and cannot be dealt with using savings outside of the Section 457 plan. Imminent foreclosure, eviction, uninsured medical or funeral expenses or an uninsured casualty loss are examples of unforeseeable emergencies. *This is a high barrier to access.* Don't plan on being able to get the money until you leave the job or reach retirement age. Deferred compensation is a supplemental retirement plan; consider it as such.

BEFORE YOU NEED THE MONEY, SHOULD YOU STAY WHERE YOU ARE OR USE THE IRA ROLLOVER OPTION?

At the time you retire, you may not need any of the proceeds of your Section 457 account. If you leave the money in place, your balance continues to grow on a tax-deferred basis. If you don't want to begin drawing the money at retirement, the only decision to be made is whether or not you want to leave your balance with your employer's deferred compensation plan or roll it over into an existing or new Individual Retirement Account (IRA).

> **There is a good case for leaving the money where it is** if you are satisfied with the Chicago Park's 457 plan: the investment options that are offered, the fees, the customer service provided by the administrator, the continued oversight by your employer and union, and the opportunity to discuss the plan with your

active and retired coworkers. If you are happy with the plan that helped you build a pretty good nest egg, why change?

There is a case for rolling the money into an IRA if you are not totally satisfied with your employer's plan, you'd like to consolidate your investments with another company or advisor, or you want to make some distributions to charities though an IRA permitted "Qualified Charitable Distribution (QCD)."

A word of caution is in order regarding the 10% penalty that is paid when money is withdrawn from an IRA before age 59-1/2. Your municipal 457 plan does not have a 10% penalty for withdrawal before age 59-1/2. Whenever you take out Section 457 money you pay only the tax. But IRAs and a new employer's 401(k) plan *do* have such a penalty. If you roll Section 457 money into a plan that has such a rule, your 457 money will be subject to a 10% penalty if withdrawn before age 59-1/2. For this reason, it might be better to leave your balance with the deferred compensation plan administrator until you are ready to begin distributions or at least until after age 59-1/2.

There is a lot of good information available from general sources to help you make the rollover/don't-rollover decision.

Rolling your money over into an IRA and then converting the IRA to a Roth IRA is a related strategy, again beyond the scope of this book. But there is considerable information and advice available on this subject.

WHEN YOU NEED THE MONEY

Prior to age 73, you have considerable flexibility regarding withdrawal of funds. As retirement approaches, you should be in contact with your plan administrator to go over your options. Taking all your money out at once is certainly allowed. This is the so-called "lump sum option," but you'll possibly skyrocket into a high tax bracket if you do this. Not a good idea.

You may want to choose a series of systematic withdrawals paid on a set schedule (month, quarter, year). While the money is being paid out, your balance stays invested as you have directed.

Or you may choose some other schedule. When that time comes, check out your options. Again, your balance always stays invested as you directed while you are drawing out the money.

There is a lot written about how much a retiree can safely draw out of a defined contribution retirement plan and not run out of money during his or her life. Since public employee deferred compensation plans are supplemental to a pension (in the case of Illinois, a modified-inflation-adjusted pension), the rate of withdrawal is not critical as it is for a person in a 401(k)-only retirement environment. Again, there is a lot written on this subject and it is easily available.

REQUIRED MINIMUM DISTRIBUTIONS

However, beginning at age 73, if you are no longer working for the Chicago Park District, you must begin withdrawals that meet or exceed so-called Required Minimum Distributions (RMD). Essentially the RMD is an annual amount calculated with the intent that most of the account balance will be withdrawn during the remaining life of the participant. The plan administrator can advise you of how the RMD schedule will work. You can also look directly at the approved IRS schedule at irs.gov or simply Google "RMD table." The age 73 requirement for RMDs changes to age 75 in 2033.

Here is a quick example. At the date of publication of this book, an age 73 retiree with a $200,000 account balance must withdraw at least $7,550 that year. At age 81, an account balance of $200,000 would trigger a minimum withdrawal of $10,300. These numbers will vary in the future.

If you do not live long enough to draw out a large part of your balance, there is no penalty associated with this. Any balance left when you die passes to your heirs and the tax liability is transferred to the next owner (possibly with different withdrawal rules). Your beneficiary pays the tax when the money is withdrawn.

Work closely with your IRA custodian or 457 plan administrator to ensure you are following RMD rules.

THE ANNUITY OPTION

Before or after age 73, there is the opportunity to purchase an **annuity** to pay you (or you and your spouse) a monthly amount for life. Under this option, your balance does *not* stay invested as you direct. The annuity company takes all the money in exchange for the promise to pay the annuity each month as long as you live. If you live a short time, they win. If you live until 102, *you* win. There are also some variations where you can guarantee that a minimum number of payments will be made to your survivors even if you don't live a long time.

When you buy an annuity, you are really transferring investment risk and mortality risk (*i.e.,* how long you are going to live) to an insurance company. Some private sector retirees may want to do this. If a person was self-employed and sold a business in retirement for $3 million, he or she might reasonably consider using some of that money to buy an annuity. Since that retiree does not have a pension, the annuity that is purchased acts in many ways just like a pension.

But not many public service retirees choose annuities to withdraw money from their deferred compensation plan. You already have a guaranteed income for life (the Chicago Parks PEABF pension) with some level of inflation protection. You likely also have a small Social Security benefit coming. So, it's reasonably safe for a parks retiree to accept the investment and mortality risk of their deferred compensation account as opposed to transferring that risk to an insurance company (and incurring the insurance contract's attendant fees and profits).

But if you want to check out an annuity option, check it out!

DEFERRED COMPENSATION SUMMARY

A public employee can place a considerable amount of personal savings into a deferred compensation account. This approach will beat savings outside the account in the long term. There are a broad range of diversified asset classes that can be chosen and mixed to create excellent long-term gains. Participants should understand these investments well enough to make appropriate allocation decisions. If you are not in that position, you can improve your own knowledge and/or work with the deferred compensation company or a personal advisor to assist you. Rebalancing your account regularly or even from time to time adds value. Deferred compensation accounts can also be put on a sort of "automatic pilot" as there are opportunities for preset, age-appropriate investing and rebalancing. There is a lot of flexibility in withdrawing money, but moderately sized withdrawals must occur at age 73 and grow after that age.

THOUGHTS THAT DIDN'T FIT ANYWHERE ELSE

Section 457 plans are very popular where they have been introduced. And, these plans were popular under the *old* rules, which restricted withdrawal options and treated account balances as the property of an employer. With the 1996 and 2000 reforms, interest in 457 plan participation grew. The tax break on contributions, access to the broad investment markets for a small deposit and the convenience of payroll deduction make these plans an excellent "third leg" of the retirement stool.

The dollars that go into deferred compensation will end up in competition with other expense and savings needs: buying a house, saving for kids' college, and other requirements of life. It's hard to max out every year and still feed your family. So don't worry when your first child is born and your spouse cuts back at work. You will probably need to drop your contribution to deferred compensation. Keep everything in balance. But remember that magical time value of compounded earnings. Don't let deferred compensation sit too long on the back burner. The best approach: start deferring as soon as you are eligible.

WHAT ELSE CAN YOU DO TO IMPROVE YOUR DEFERRED SAVINGS?

There are a range of further actions you can consider. Or not. Many of the readers already have a good grasp of their deferred compensation personal savings plan.

Of course, if you are not saving in deferred compensation, strongly consider joining the plan.

If you are enrolled in deferred compensation and would like to improve this leg of your retirement income, you can do a little or a lot. Reread this chapter. Visit your plan administrator's website at empower.com or call 1-800-701-8255. Consider the two recommended books by Dr. Bernstein or find something similar. Maybe a relative or a friend has a decent financial planning or retirement book.

Rebalance your account if it hasn't been done since the 1990s. Be sure you understand your investments and statements. If you don't understand them, plan a meeting with the deferred compensation representative. Take ownership.

SECTION ENDNOTES

To arrive at the 23.1% tax rate imputed for "Tim's" savings outside of deferred compensation, the following was used: a blended the capital gains/dividend rate for three-quarters of his investment earnings with a typical top rate of 28%, then added 4.95 percentage points for Illinois tax.

APPENDIX

CONTRIBUTORS

Daniel W. Ryan

IPPFA and Retired Finance Director and Benefits Administrator

Dan is retired from careers as a municipal finance director and union benefit administrator and is a longtime trustee of the Skokie police pension fund. His research and writings on Social Security and public pensions have been referenced in pension fund newsletters and newspapers nationwide, including the *Wall Street Journal*. He is a part-time project coordinator for IPPFA.

Michael K. Lappe

IPPFA and Retired Chicago Police

Mike is a former Chicago Police officer who retired from CPD after more than 38 years of experience. Critically injured in a shooting incident, Mike rehabbed himself and returned to limited duty. He currently serves as an elected retirement board trustee for the Chicago police pension fund and is a past adjunct professor in criminal justice. He has a master's degree in public safety administration and is considered an expert in disability pensions for police officers. Mike is a part-time staff associate for the Illinois Public Pension Fund Association (IPPFA).

James McNamee

IPPFA

Born in Chicago, Jim McNamee began his career in public service in 1979 as a police officer for the Village of Barrington. In 1983, Mr. McNamee was elected to the Barrington Police Pension Board as a trustee. During his term as trustee, he quickly saw the need for training and education on pension matters. Taking action, Mr. McNamee went to work to form what would become the Illinois Public Pension Fund Association.

IPPFA Association Office
Administrative assistance was provided by IPPFA office staff Julie Guy, Mandy Paciorkowski, and Madeline Lusted.

ADDITIONAL ACKNOWLEDGMENTS

The Trustees, Executive Director Steve Swanson, and the employees of the Chicago Park District pension office provided valuable information for this book, and their help is greatly appreciated.

Former Executive Director Dean Niedospial also provided insight.

Photography assistance on IPPFA publications provided by Frank Alatorre, Chicago Police Department

Made in the USA
Monee, IL
04 November 2026

67380143R00049